The Rainforest

Richard Jones

Illustrated by
Shirley Wheeler

Studio Editions

**To the Forests of the Earth –
that they survive**

First published in 1993 by Studio Editions Ltd,
Princess House, 50 Eastcastle Street,
London W1N 7AP, England.

Text and illustrations copyright © 1993
Studio Editions

ISBN 1 85170 872 3

Printed and bound in Singapore

Contents

What is a Rainforest?

The **Rainforest** is a dark and gloomy place. The leaves are dripping with water, and the ground is soft and squelchy underfoot. Sinister dark shapes loom in the undergrowth.

Well, that is one way of looking at a rainforest. Here is another.

Vast tree trunks rise like the columns of a grand cathedral to the leafy roof above. The air is alive with the calls of birds and insects.

Overhead the world is a riot of colourful birds and flowers and green leaves shimmering in the sunshine.

Huge bright butterflies flap lazily through the trees. Vines and creepers swing from every branch.

Rainforests have existed for millions of years. They contain a bewildering number of plants and animals that have developed together to form a complex *environment*.

We still do not know how many types of plants and animals there are in the forests, but it could be as many as 25 million different *species*, most of which we have still to discover.

Rainforests are the most astonishing places on Earth.

Rainforest Life

When explorers first trekked into the forests they found whole new tribes of people living deep in the jungle. Tribespeople made, and still make, their clothes, shelter and tools from forest materials. They gather berries, nuts and fruit and hunt animals for their skins and meat.

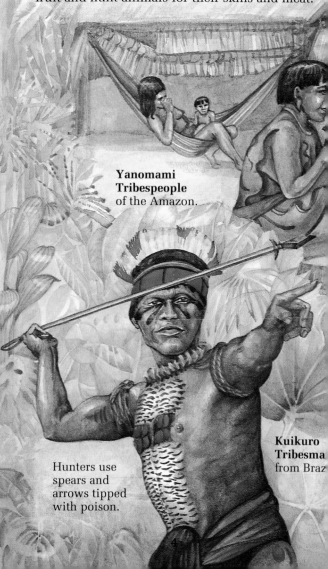

Yanomami Tribespeople of the Amazon.

Kuikuro Tribesma from Braz

Hunters use spears and arrows tipped with poison.

4

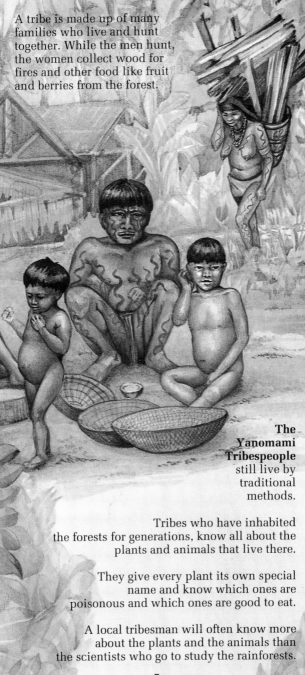

A tribe is made up of many families who live and hunt together. While the men hunt, the women collect wood for fires and other food like fruit and berries from the forest.

The Yanomami Tribespeople still live by traditional methods.

Tribes who have inhabited the forests for generations, know all about the plants and animals that live there.

They give every plant its own special name and know which ones are poisonous and which ones are good to eat.

A local tribesman will often know more about the plants and the animals than the scientists who go to study the rainforests.

Rainforest Tribes

The rainforests have probably been inhabited for thousands of years, although no-one knows exactly how or when the first people started to live there. Our only clues are a few fragments of broken pottery.

Tribes still use the mud from the forests to make clay pots, jars and ornaments. They also use the wood, bark and leaves of the rainforest to make baskets, masks and carvings. Each tribe has its own style of decoration.

Drums are made from hollowed logs and animals skins.

The **Iban** of Sarawak and the **Dyak** of Borneo use the **slash and burn** method of temporary farming. They cut down trees and clear a small area, then burn the undergrowth to kill the weeds. They plant crops which they tend and harvest. When the regrowing forest plants get too strong, they move to a new part of the forest and start again.

Paints, made from plant colours and mud, are used with feathers to decorate face and hair, for ceremonies and special occasions.

The **Malaysian Semang** use a blowpipe made from one particular type of bamboo pole. With this, they shoot down monkeys and birds, using a dart tipped with poison from the skin of a poison arrow frog.

By farming only small areas, and by leaving the tree stumps and roots, they do no lasting damage to the forest. Modern farming destroys the forest completely.

Layers of the Rainforest

High above the ground, the tops of the trees form a network of branches and leaves called the **Canopy**. A few giant-sized trees, **Emergents**, stand out above the canopy.

EPIPHYTES
Many trees are covered with *epiphytes.* These small plants, such as ferns and orchids wrap their roots around the branches of trees, rather than down in the ground.

By doing this they can get more sunlight than plants growing beneath the trees at ground level.

EMERGENTS
Some great trees like
the giant **Eucalyptus** of
Australia stand out
even taller, above
the canopy.

CANOPY
The **Canopy** is like
a ceiling and the vast
tree trunks are like
columns holding it up.

UNDERSTOREY
Far down beneath the
canopy, the foliage
of the tall trees has
blocked out most sunlight.
Here in the **Understorey**
it is much darker.

UNDERGROWTH
Tall trees prevent
the sunlight reaching the
Undergrowth leaving
it for ever in the
shade.

Few plants grow
among the twisted tree
roots on the dark forest floor. Where
a little sunshine does break through,
herbs and bushes form a thick tangle.

Any fruits or seeds falling down from the trees
above are quickly eaten by animals or carried off
by ants to their nests.

9

The Undergrowth

Deep in the rainforest, the soil is poor in *nutrients* and little grows on the ground. To get nourishment, trees extend a tangled mat of long shallow roots. Instead of strong, deep roots supporting the weight of the towering trunks, trees have large buttress roots.

Animals like the **Chequered Elephant Shrew** feed on seeds and fruits falling down from the trees up above.

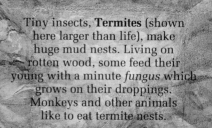

Tiny insects, **Termites** (shown here larger than life), make huge mud nests. Living on rotten wood, some feed their young with a minute *fungus* which grows on their droppings. Monkeys and other animals like to eat termite nests.

Fungi grow on almost anything that the insects and animals do not eat. Here a fungus makes the perfect shelter for the **Poison Arrow Frog**.

10

The **Bush Cricket** usually avoids detection by looking like a dead leaf. It also warns off its enemies by flashing open its wings to reveal two startling eye spots.

The **Passenger-Carrying Poison Frog** carries its tadpole on its back.

Even **Crabs** live in the rainforest, *scavenging* for their food on the forest floor.

Animals and Birds of the Undergrowth

In the dark dense gloom of the forest floor, creatures feed on leaves, roots and berries, keeping watch for attacks from other animals.

Dark-coated animals like the **Agouti** and the **Peccary** of South and Central America, blend into this shadowy world.

Large cats are the most dangerous of *predators.* As they stalk through the dense sun-dappled *undergrowth,* the stripes of the **Tiger** and the spots of the **Jaguar** help to disguise them.

Deep inside the jungles of the Indonesian island of Sumatra lives the secretive **Sumatran Rhinoceros.** Only a few of these shy creatures are thought still to exist.

In the rainforests of Africa, **Gorillas** live in groups of 10-20 animals. In spite of their huge size and ferocious chest-beating, gorillas are peaceful creatures, feeding on leaves and fruit.

The **Mandrill,** a kind of baboon from West Africa, is brilliantly coloured.

The **Bowerbird** and the **Cassowary** live in the forest undergrowth of Australia and New Guinea.

The male **Bowerbird** builds a nest or bower on the ground, decorating it with flowers, berries and stones to attract a mate.

The flightless **Cassowary** pushes its way through the thick undergrowth with its bony 'helmet'.

Plants and Insects of the Undergrowth

Despite their strong **Buttress Roots**, trees do fall over, letting sunlight through the canopy at last. Soon the trees rot down.

Huge **Beetle Grubs** eat the logs.

Fungi develop on the rotting wood and leaves.

Seeds which have been *dormant* for months, or years, now start to grow. Soon the forest clearing is a scrambling mass of lush growth.

The bright colours of **Caterpillars** are a warning to predators that they are poisonous.

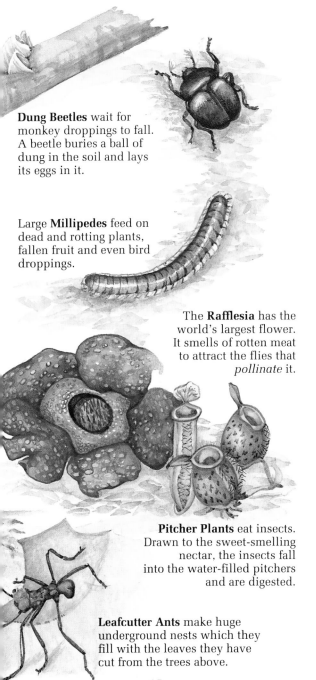

Dung Beetles wait for monkey droppings to fall. A beetle buries a ball of dung in the soil and lays its eggs in it.

Large **Millipedes** feed on dead and rotting plants, fallen fruit and even bird droppings.

The **Rafflesia** has the world's largest flower. It smells of rotten meat to attract the flies that *pollinate* it.

Pitcher Plants eat insects. Drawn to the sweet-smelling nectar, the insects fall into the water-filled pitchers and are digested.

Leafcutter Ants make huge underground nests which they fill with the leaves they have cut from the trees above.

15

The Understorey

The **Understorey** is dominated by tall tree trunks. Towering above is the **Canopy** with its branches and leaves blocking out the light. Down below lies the forest floor, the **Undergrowth**.

Few flowers and leaves grow here in the understorey, except those of young trees and plants struggling to reach the light high up in the canopy.

The **Pygmy Marmoset** chews holes in the tree trunks, and drinks the sweet juices of the sap that seeps out.

The **Flying Lizard** extends its fan-like sails to glide through the air.

Vines and creepers stretch from tree to tree in a twisted maze.

Termites make their blob-shaped nests out of mud. Their mud-covered routes to the ground wind down the trees like veins.

The **Sugar Glider** of Australia is really a type of possum, with bat-like *membranes* between its legs.

Most bats roost high in the trees, but **Tent Bats** live nearer the ground. They chew through nerves of a large leaf which then folds over to make a neat tent for daytime sleeping.

Animals and Birds of the Understorey

To move around in the *understorey,* animals use the long branches like pathways through the trees. Or they sit and wait for their prey.

Orang-utans, from Sumatra and Borneo, feed on leaves and berries. Although the mothers carry their young around with them, these great apes usually live alone.

Chimpanzees live in groups in the forests of Central West Africa. Unlike most other monkeys and apes they use tools; a stick for instance to pick out tasty termites from their holes.

Ocelots, inhabiting the forests of Central and South America, hunt alone or in pairs during the night and rest during the day. The **Ocelot** catches lizards, snakes, agouti and other small animals by jumping down from a branch as they pass underneath.

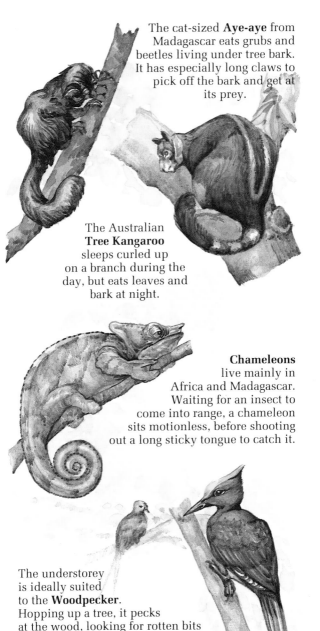

The cat-sized **Aye-aye** from Madagascar eats grubs and beetles living under tree bark. It has especially long claws to pick off the bark and get at its prey.

The Australian **Tree Kangaroo** sleeps curled up on a branch during the day, but eats leaves and bark at night.

Chameleons live mainly in Africa and Madagascar. Waiting for an insect to come into range, a chameleon sits motionless, before shooting out a long sticky tongue to catch it.

The understorey is ideally suited to the **Woodpecker**. Hopping up a tree, it pecks at the wood, looking for rotten bits of bark with insects living underneath. In order to cling to a tree it has especially large feet, with long sharp claws.

19

Plants and Insects of the Understorey

In the **Understorey**, **Vines** and **Creepers** wind themselves around the trunks of trees. Plants known as **Epiphytes**, grow on the trunks and branches, often with their roots dangling in the air.

Stingless **Trigona Bees** make their nests in a hollow branch. They use mud to extend the entrance into a long tube.

The **Bromeliad** is an epiphyte. Filled with water, it makes an ideal home for a tadpole. The parent frog visits the plant and drops in an insect for its offspring.

Beautiful **Orchid Flowers** hang down from a knot of roots around a branch.

An **Indian Leaf Butterfly** resting with folded wings on a tree trunk looks like a dead leaf. But, as it flies, the colours of its upper surface flash brightly, to confuse any birds chasing it.

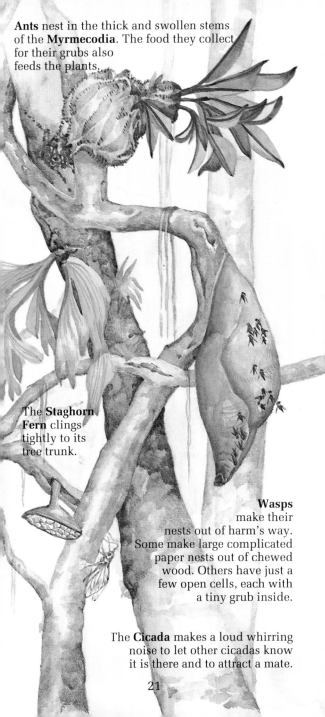

Ants nest in the thick and swollen stems of the **Myrmecodia**. The food they collect for their grubs also feeds the plants.

The **Staghorn Fern** clings tightly to its tree trunk.

Wasps make their nests out of harm's way. Some make large complicated paper nests out of chewed wood. Others have just a few open cells, each with a tiny grub inside.

The **Cicada** makes a loud whirring noise to let other cicadas know it is there and to attract a mate.

21

The Canopy

It is in the great crowns of the trees of the **Canopy** that most of the rainforest creatures live. High up, the forest is a blaze of colour, its thick *foliage* providing food and shelter for a dazzling array of wildlife.

Here there are always different trees in flower, different fruits for the monkeys to eat, and new nuts for the birds to crack open.

Great **Fruit Bats** set off at dusk in search of fruit and flowers. During the day they roost in the high branches.

A brightly coloured **Praying Mantis** looks just like a flower, but it kills and eats any insect unfortunate enough to settle upon it.

An **Eagle**, flying over the tallest trees of all, the *emergents,* watches out for his prey.

Huge **Bird-Wing Butterflies** flutter in the sunshine. The males are bright black and green, but the females are brown.

The **Potto** feeds at night on fruit and also eats any insects which it comes across.

Tree Snakes, *camouflaged* against the greenery, make themselves at home in the foliage.

Animals of the Canopy

High up in the treetops of the *canopy*, the trees form an almost continuous web of leaves and branches. Different animals use different ways to move about.

The **Colobus Monkey** from Africa makes giant leaps between branches, using its strong legs to push off and its tail to balance.

The **Gibbon**, which inhabits the forests of South Asia, uses its long arms to swing from bough to bough.

There are slow-moving creatures too, like the **Loris** from South-East Asia. By day it hides in tree hollows or clings to a branch, head tucked between its back legs. By night it climbs carefully up a branch to snatch at a passing lizard or an insect.

The **Spider Monkey** of Central and South America uses its tail like a fifth leg, curling it around a branch and hanging down to feed.

Sloths spend almost all their lives hanging upside down in the canopies of Central and South America. When they travel they move very slowly using their long curved claws to grip on to branches. *Algae* growing on the hairs of the sloth makes its fur look green.

The **Tree Pangolin** or 'Scaly Anteater' from Africa and South Asia uses its strong claws to break open the nests of termites and ants. Its hard scales protect it from bites and stings.

Birds and Insects of the Canopy

The **Canopy** is home to a fantastic variety of birds and insects, feeding on either the leaves, the flowers, the fruit, or on each other.

Hummingbirds live in the Americas. Hovering beside a flower, a bird sips *nectar* with its long tongue.

Blue Morpho Butterflies from Central and South America glisten in the sunshine. The special scales on their wings make them appear blue one minute and silver the next.

Huge **Eagles** perch on the high branches of the tall trees or soar above the forest in search of their prey. They dive without warning to snatch up a monkey, bat or bird in their sharp claws.

The **Golden Beetle** from Central America looks as if it is made of brilliant metal. It flies from flower to flower high up in the trees.

Brightly coloured **Macaws**, found in the American tropics, use their strong curved beaks to crack open hard nuts and seeds. Like other species in the parrot family, they mate for life, and both parents look after the young.

The **Toucan**, also from the American tropics, rips open fruit with its huge beak and picks out the soft centre.

Birds of Paradise inhabit New Guinea and Australia. The male birds are decorated with gaudy feathers and display themselves to impress the female birds.

27

Rainforest Rivers

In the rainforests, falling rain trickles down between the tree roots forming small **Rivulets**; these become **Streams** and streams become **Rivers**. Eventually the rivers flow into the **Sea**.

Some vast rivers, like the **Amazon** and the **Niger**, are wide and slow-moving. As they reach the sea, they break up into a network of channels, called a **Delta**, with sand banks and islands in between.

A **Blue-Eared Kingfisher** is about to dive into the water to snatch up a fish in its beak.

The **Bouto** or 'Amazon Porpoise' is related to dolphins.

A **Dragonfly** rests on a reed stem.

The **Giant Water Lily** has huge round leaves.

The **Hatchet Fish** jumps up to catch its prey.

Pirhana Fish have strong jaws and teeth. In spite of their reputation as meat eaters, most types feed on seeds and berries which have fallen into the water.

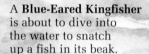

The banks of the river are hidden from view by the overhanging branches of the trees which almost touch the water. A **Rufous-Backed Kingfisher** sits here for a moment.

Herons can be seen fishing at the edge of the water.

The **Mudskipper Fish** is more at home out of water than in it.

An **Archer Fish** squirts water to knock insects down into its waiting jaws.

The muddy islands of the delta are covered with **Mangrove Trees**. The roots grow up out of the mud so that the trees can breathe.

29

Destruction of the Rainforest

The people who have lived in the rainforest all their lives are being displaced by settlers moving in. Their axes and spears, which did no lasting damage to the forest, are being replaced by chainsaws, bulldozers and guns.

Huge quarries are excavated as gold, silver and other valuable metals are discovered. Oil wells are drilled.

Farmers can now travel on the new roads deep into the interior of the forests. There they plant crops and graze cattle after burning down the trees.

If the rainforests are to survive, governments, mining and timber companies will have to change the ways they harvest the forest. Farmers, too, must learn about their forests so that they do not destroy the soil.

The trees are cut down
for their valuable wood.

With the trees gone, the
rains wash away the soil
and the rivers become
clogged with mud.

Roads are built
so that lorries
can carry the
logs away.

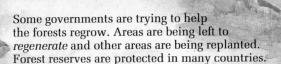

Some governments are trying to help
the forests regrow. Areas are being left to
regenerate and other areas are being replanted.
Forest reserves are protected in many countries.

The rainforests of the world are still
disappearing fast. The more we learn about
the forests, the more we can do to help save
them from complete and final destruction.

Glossary

Algae Microscopic green plants.

Camouflaged Coloured like a leaf or twig.

Canopy Top-most branches and leaves of the trees.

Dormant Hidden, waiting to move or grow.

Delta Network of channels and muddy islands at the mouth of a river.

Emergent One of the very tall trees which stick out above the canopy.

Environment A collection of animals and plants living together.

Epiphyte A plant which grows on other plants.

Foliage Leaves.

Fungus Toadstool or other related plant which feeds on rotten wood.

Nectar Sweet liquid from flowers.

Nutrients The chemicals which make up foods.

Pollinate Move pollen from one plant to another so that seeds can develop.

Predator An animal which hunts and eats other animals.

Regenerate Grow up again.

Scavenger An animal that feeds on whatever can be found lying around.

Species A type of animal or a type of plant.

Undergrowth Plants growing on the forest floor.

Understorey Tree trunks and epiphytes between the canopy and forest floor.

Pocket Pullout Series